CEC Mini-Library

Exceptional
Children At Risk

*A*buse and
Neglect of
Exceptional
Children

Cynthia L. Warger
with Stephanna Tewey
and Marjorie Megivern

Published by The Council for Exceptional Children

A Product of the ERIC Clearinghouse
on Handicapped and Gifted Children

Library of Congress Catalog Card Number 91-58303

ISBN 0-86586-208-7

A product of the ERIC / OSEP Special Project, the ERIC Clearinghouse on Handicapped and Gifted Children

Published in 1991 by The Council for Exceptional Children, 1920 Association Drive, Reston, Virginia 22091-1589
Stock No. P351

This publication was prepared with funding from the U.S. Department of Education, Office of Special Education Programs, contract no. RI88062007. Contractors undertaking such projects under government sponsorship are encouraged to express freely their judgment in professional and technical matters. Prior to publication the manuscript was submitted for critical review and determination of professional competence. This publication has met such standards. Points of view, however, do not necessarily represent the official view or opinions of either The Council for Exceptional Children or the Department of Education.

Printed in the United States of America
10   9   8   7   6   5   4   3   2   1

Contents

It is estimated that 1 million children are abused annually, and many of these children have disabilities. Many special educators are concerned with all children who are abused since they require additional attention and support to overcome disabling effects of abuse.

Types of abuse include physical and mental injury, sexual abuse or exploitation, negligent treatment, and maltreatment of children. Each state has a legal definition of abuse. Children with disabilities have been found to comprise a disproportionate number of child abuse cases, and special issues arise in cases that involve both sexual abuse and disabilities. Some factors associated with parents who abuse their children have been identified. It is unclear whether children who have disabilities are at greater risk of being abused, but there are certainly cases in which abuse has created physical disabilities and health problems.

Educators are in a unique position to identify and report behaviors symptomatic of abuse and neglect. Variations in state laws and reporting requirements result in variations in districts' referral processes.

Steps for establishing effective reporting procedures have been identified. Preventative measures include school programs and support for parents of children with disabilities, preventative programs for students, and measures for preventing institutional abuse and abuse by school staff.

Foreword

EXCEPTIONAL CHILDREN AT RISK
CEC Mini-Library

Many of today's pressing social problems, such as poverty, homelessness, drug abuse, and child abuse, are factors that place children and youth at risk in a variety of ways. There is a growing need for special educators to understand the risk factors that students must face and, in particular, the risks confronting children and youth who have been identified as exceptional. A child may be at risk *due to* a number of quite different phenomena, such as poverty or abuse. Therefore, the child may be at risk *for* a variety of problems, such as developmental delays; debilitating physical illnesses or psychological disorders; failing or dropping out of school; being incarcerated; or generally having an unrewarding, unproductive adulthood. Compounding the difficulties that both the child and the educator face in dealing with these risk factors is the unhappy truth that a child may have more than one risk factor, thereby multiplying his or her risk and need.

The struggle within special education to address these issues was the genesis of the 1991 CEC conference "Children on the Edge." The content for the conference strands is represented by this series of publications, which were developed through the assistance of the Division of Innovation and Development of the U.S. Office of Special Education Programs (OSEP). OSEP funds the ERIC/OSEP Special Project, a research dissemination activity of The Council for Exceptional Children. As a part of its publication program, which synthesizes and translates research in special education for a variety of audiences, the ERIC/OSEP Special Project coordinated the development of this series of books and assisted in their dissemination to special education practitioners.

Each book in the series pertains to one of the conference strands. Each provides a synthesis of the literature in its area, followed by practical suggestions—derived from the literature—for program developers, administrators, and teachers. The 11 books in the series are as follows:

- *Programming for Aggressive and Violent Students* addresses issues that educators and other professionals face in contending with episodes of violence and aggression in the schools.

- *Abuse and Neglect of Exceptional Children* examines the role of the special educator in dealing with children who are abused and neglected and those with suspected abuse and neglect.

- *Special Health Care in the School* provides a broad-based definition of the population of students with special health needs and discusses their unique educational needs.

- *Homeless and in Need of Special Education* examines the plight of the fastest growing segment of the homeless population, families with children.

- *Hidden Youth: Dropouts from Special Education* addresses the difficulties of comparing and drawing meaning from dropout data prepared by different agencies and examines the characteristics of students and schools that place students at risk for leaving school prematurely.

- *Born Substance Exposed, Educationally Vulnerable* examines what is known about the long-term effects of exposure *in utero* to alcohol and other drugs, as well as the educational implications of those effects.

- *Depression and Suicide: Special Education Students at Risk* reviews the role of school personnel in detecting signs of depression and potential suicide and in taking appropriate action, as well as the role of the school in developing and implementing treatment programs for this population.

- *Language Minority Students with Disabilities* discusses the preparation needed by schools and school personnel to meet the needs of limited-English-proficient students with disabilities.

- *Alcohol and Other Drugs: Use, Abuse, and Disabilities* addresses the issues involved in working with children and adolescents who have disabling conditions and use alcohol and other drugs.

- *Rural, Exceptional, At Risk* examines the unique difficulties of delivering education services to at-risk children and youth with exceptionalities who live in rural areas.

- *Double Jeopardy: Pregnant and Parenting Youth in Special Education* addresses the plight of pregnant teenagers and teenage parents, especially those in special education, and the role of program developers and practitioners in responding to their educational needs.

Background information applicable to the conference strand on juvenile corrections can be found in another publication, *Special Education in Juvenile Corrections,* which is a part of the CEC Mini-Library *Working with Behavioral Disorders.* That publication addresses the demographics of incarcerated youth and promising practices in responding to their needs.

1. Introduction

It is estimated that 1 million children are abused annually, and many of these children have disabilities. Many special educators are concerned with all children who are abused since they require additional attention and support to overcome disabling effects of abuse.

Four-year-old Brian has wandered, once again, unsupervised from his home. It is near midnight, and he is frightened. He crawls into a drainage pipe under an overpass and cries as the cars whiz by overhead.

Six-year-old Deanna cries when her teacher asks her to sit. The night before, her stepfather tied her hands with a dirty kitchen rag, blindfolded her, and forced himself sexually on her.

Harlan cowers from the teacher when she asks about the series of burns on the back of his neck. He claims that a match accidentally fell on him.

Why would a parent or adult intentionally cause any one of these maladies to happen in a child? What kind of society permits child maltreatment? If we knew the answer to these questions, we could effectively intervene to stop the pain and suffering that happens nationwide each year to more than an estimated 1 million children, many of whom are disabled (National Center on Child Abuse and Neglect, 1988).

Child abuse, broadly defined as willful behavior by parents or guardians that harms a child in their care (Garbarino, 1987b), is not a new phenomenon; yet our knowledge about how to prevent and effectively intervene to stop abuse is limited. We know that abusers come from all socioeconomic, racial, religious, and ethnic groups (Mullins, 1986), but beyond that, we cannot be too conclusive. Fortunately, over the past two decades we have expanded our understanding of child abuse and neglect. We have some answers.

For many special educators, all abused children, with or without disabilities, are considered to be special. They require additional support and attention to overcome the potentially disabling effects of the abuse. Special educators can play a crucial role in preventing child abuse, as well as in reporting and supporting victims of child abuse.

This book is intended to provide special educators with an overview of what we know about child abuse. It first describes what we know from the research and professional literature about child abuse generally and, specifically, as it relates to those children with disabilities. A look at some of the factors associated with abuse follows. Finally, the book offers strategies to assist educators in combating abuse in their schools and lists available resources.

2. Synthesis of Research

Types of abuse include physical and mental injury, sexual abuse or exploitation, negligent treatment, and maltreatment of children. Each state has a legal definition of abuse. Children with disabilities have been found to comprise a disproportionate number of child abuse cases, and special issues arise in cases that involve both sexual abuse and disabilities. Some factors associated with parents who abuse their children have been identified. It is unclear whether children who have disabilities are at greater risk of being abused, but there are certainly cases in which abuse has created physical disabilities and health problems.

Definition

Throughout history, pain—both physical and emotional—has been inflicted on children. Children have been killed for being "defective" or "unruly," beaten with rods and belts for misbehavior, forced to work under unsafe and unsanitary conditions, and left to starve (Kline, 1977). Not until the 1940s, however, did child abuse become recognized as a medical phenomenon. It took another 20 years for child abuse to gain public recognition. In what now is considered to be the pivotal event marking public concern with the consequences of child abuse, Kempe and his colleagues (1962) coined the term *battered child syndrome*, to refer to a clinical condition in young children who present a variety of severe injuries, including fractures of any bone, subdural hematoma, failure to thrive, soft tissue swellings, or skin bruising, which are intentionally caused by a parent or foster parent. With the naming of this syndrome, physical abuse of children was now identified as a medical condition, complete with symptoms and a cause.

It took another decade for the term to find its way into the legal arena, in the form of The Child Abuse Prevention and Treatment Act of 1974 (Public Law 93-247). Amended in 1984 under P.L. 100-294 (The Child Abuse Prevention, Adoption, and Family Services Act), the act defines child abuse and neglect as the physical or mental injury, sexual abuse or exploitation, negligent treatment, or maltreatment of children under the age of 18 by a person who is responsible for the child's welfare under circumstances indicating that the child's health or welfare is harmed or threatened thereby. As a result of the Child Abuse Amendments of 1984 (P.L. 98-457), child abuse also includes the withholding of medical treatment for an infant's life-threatening conditions.

Types of Child Abuse

The term *child abuse* has been applied to forms of physical abuse, child neglect, sexual abuse, and emotional maltreatment. A description of each, prepared by the National Center on Child Abuse and Neglect (1989), follows.

Physical Abuse. Physical abuse is characterized by inflicting physical injury by punching, beating, kicking, biting, burning, or otherwise harming a child. Although the injury is not an accident, the parent or caretaker may not have intended to hurt the child.

Child Neglect. Child neglect is characterized by failure to provide for the child's basic needs. Neglect can be physical, educational, or emotional. Physical neglect includes refusal of or delay in seeking health care, abandonment, expulsion from home or not allowing a runaway to return home, and inadequate supervision. Educational neglect includes permission of chronic truancy, failure to enroll a child of mandatory school age, and inattention to a special educational need. Emotional neglect includes such actions as chronic or extreme spouse abuse in the child's presence, permission of drug or alcohol use by the child, and refusal of or failure to provide needed psychological care.

Sexual Abuse. Sexual abuse includes fondling a child's genitals, intercourse, incest, rape, sodomy, exhibitionism, and sexual exploitation. To be considered child abuse, these acts have to be committed by a parent responsible for the care of a child.

Emotional Maltreatment. This form of child abuse and neglect includes acts or omissions by the parents that have caused, or could cause, serious behavioral, cognitive, emotional, or mental disorders.

Psychological maltreatment is a concerted attack on the development of self and social competence. Five forms of psychological maltreatment have been discussed in the literature:

- Rejecting: the refusal to acknowledge the child's worth and needs.
- Isolating: cutting off the child from normal social experiences.

- Terrorizing: verbally assaulting the child or creating a climate of fear.

- Ignoring: being psychologically unavailable.

- Corrupting: socializing the child to engage in destructive behavior and reinforcing the deviance (Garbarino, 1987a).

Each of these forms of emotional or psychological maltreatment can have significant implications for school functioning. According to Garbarino (1987a), intellectual functioning, social competence, and emotional development all can be affected.

Problems Defining Child Abuse

To carry out the legal mandates of federal law, every state has at least one legal definition of child abuse and neglect in its laws to establish official reporting procedures and to define jurisdiction (National Center on Child Abuse and Neglect, 1984). Local agencies, which carry out state mandates as they relate to child abuse laws, also generally develop operational definitions for reporting and accepting cases, which may or may not mirror state definitions.

Most definitions of child abuse and neglect describe the parent or caretaker's unacceptable acts or omissions, the intent behind the acts or omissions, and the harmful effect to the child of those acts or omissions (National Center on Child Abuse and Neglect, 1984). It is difficult to standardize such a definition. For example, society grants parents certain basic rights, such as the right to raise their children in accordance with their personal and religious beliefs, in the privacy of their own home, and with the understanding that they are to make decisions for their children until their children are of legal age. Child abuse and neglect laws, by their nature, restrict these rights by making it illegal for parents or caretakers to harm or threaten their children. Thus, how harm or threat is defined will depend to some extent on the prevailing *community* values and attitudes regarding adequate child care and protection (National Center on Child Abuse and Neglect, 1984).

Child abuse and neglect are difficult to define, with as many definitions as there are professionals. Operating with no standard definition or, as some have described, an ambiguous definition at best, puts the educator in a precarious position—namely, how to intervene on behalf of a child suspected of being a victim of child abuse or neglect without violating the legal rights of the parent or adult caretaker (Jaeckle, 1986). In families where physical discipline is more intense and frequent, as Spinetta and Rigler (1972) found to be true in many families of lower socioeconomic status, making a case for abuse can be tenuous, at best.

Before taking any steps when child abuse is suspected, educators must understand how child abuse is legally defined in their state and locality.

Prevalence

Rising child abuse statistics have led some to question if we are becoming a society of child abusers (Bourne, 1981). According to a report conducted by the National Center on Child Abuse and Neglect (1988), over 1 million children in the United States were reported to experience demonstrable harm as a result of maltreatment in 1986, a notable 66% increase over the incidence rate estimated for 1980. In that same year, 1,100 children died as a result of abuse or neglect. In this same study, the estimate of abuse and neglect rose to 1.5 million children when the definition of abuse was expanded to include children at risk of or threatened with harm.

Other reports set child abuse statistics at a much higher rate, but as Zirpoli (1990) points out, prevalence data may vary depending on the particular study and reporting agency. Part of the difficulty in obtaining accurate data relates to the fact that prevalence reports often omit data from many states and localities, as well as use differing definitions of child abuse across localities (Zirpoli, 1986).

To complicate the situation, it is suspected that many cases of abuse go unreported (Straus, Gelles, & Steinmetz, 1980). According to Parke and Collmer (1975), child abuse might not be reported as a result of: parents not taking their abused children for medical care; parents taking their children to different doctors and facilities for medical care, making it impossible to document a pattern of abuse; the underdetection of some injuries by medical professionals; the reluctance of some doctors to report child abuse; and the tendency for public health personnel to interpret local abuse laws differently. Psychological maltreatment is seldom reported.

Even in the field of education, where it is estimated that educators see at least 50% of all abused children (National Clearinghouse on Child Abuse and Neglect, 1984), it is suspected that many cases go unreported. Part of the problem may be related to inconsistencies in definitions and enforcement procedures (McIntyre, 1990), making it difficult for educators to make definitive decisions. McIntyre (1990) also suggested that part of the problem with reporting can be related to the hierarchical relationship between teachers and principals. In those cases where principals decide not to file a report made by a teacher, teachers tend to defer to the principal's judgment (McIntyre, 1987).

Incidence of Abused Children with Disabilities

Scientifically reliable research on the incidence and prevalence of child abuse among populations with disabilities is virtually nonexistent. Possible reasons for this lack of data include relatively few empirical investigations on the topic, methodological problems related to underreporting, inaccessible data, and problems with investigation procedures (Mayer & Brenner, 1989). Differing definitions of disability and abuse also contribute to reporting problems. Little systematic investigation of the factors relating to the maltreatment of children with disabilities is particularly surprising given that children with disabilities are often overrepresented in abused and neglected samples, and that many of these children and their families have characteristics that in populations without disabilities are considered to be high-risk factors for maltreatment (Ammerman, Van Hasselt, Hersen, 1988).

Although the actual incidence of abuse of children with disabilities is unknown, estimates can be derived from studies that have looked at the proportion of a sample with regard to the disability variable. Children with disabilities have been found to comprise a disproportionate number of child abuse cases. Children with mental retardation constituted between 8% and 43% of the child abuse samples under study (Frisch & Rhoads, 1970; Martin, 1972; Morse, Sahler, & Friedman, 1970; Sandgrund, Gaines, & Green, 1974). Abnormal social behavior was noted prior to abuse for 29% of 6,000 abused children in child protective agency reports (Gil, 1970). Similarly, Johnson and Morse (1968) found that 20% of the abused children they studied were considered prior to abuse "unmanageable" by their caseworkers. In another study of psychiatrically hospitalized individuals with multiple disabilities, 39% of the sample had experienced or had a history that warranted suspicion of past or current maltreatment (Ammerman, Van Hasselt, Hersen, McGonigle, & Lubetsky, 1989).

Physical disabilities have also been associated with child abuse. In a study of children with cerebral palsy conducted by Diamond and Jaudes (1983), 20% of the sample were found to be abused. In another study, Birrell and Birrell (1968) found that 25% of a sample of abused children had physical disabilities before their abuse.

Disability and Sexual Abuse: Special Issues. Since the passage of the Child Abuse Prevention and Treatment Act of 1974 (P.L. 93-247), which included sexual abuse and exploitation in its definition of child abuse, sexual abuse has received increased attention. With regard to prevalence rates of sexual abuse among people with disabilities, research has suggested a disproportionate rate. Mayer and Brenner (1989) reported the following findings:

- Over a 7-year period, one county in Washington estimated that 3,500 individuals with disabilities had been sexually exploited.

- Case studies of 95 adults with developmental disabilities revealed that 83% of the females and 32% of the males had been sexually abused, with 45% of the abuse taking place before the victim's 18th birthday.

- Over 50% of 39 women who were blind had experienced at least one incident of forced sexual contact.

- 50% of students enrolled in the ninth grade at a residential school for the deaf reported that they had been sexually victimized.

In considering sexual abuse of people with developmental disabilities, certain fundamental issues arise. Perhaps the most problematic concerns whether a person with mental retardation is considered in the legal and practical sense to be a consenting adult. Legal debates involve the question of whether individuals can make informed decisions about sexual or other matters (Tharinger, Horton, & Miller, 1990). Furthermore, it is difficult to protect people with mental retardation from sexual abuse and exploitation while at the same time providing them with developmentally appropriate knowledge about and the fulfillment of their sexuality. Prevalence rates tend to underscore these issues and make it difficult to gauge the full impact of abuse.

Practical Problems Associating Child Abuse with People with Disabilities. Identifying the incidence of abuse with people with disabilities is difficult at best. There are real practical problems to be addressed when applying child abuse mandates to children with disabilities. A summary of these follows:

- Some children with disabilities are limited in their ability to communicate information about the abusive episode (Garbarino & Authier, 1987).

- Some children with behavioral or mental disabilities engage in self-abusive behaviors, making identification complicated (Menolascino & McCann, 1983).

- Some children with physical disabilities or mental disabilities may be prone to accidental injury, making it difficult to sort out cases of accidental from nonaccidental injuries (Garbarino & Authier, 1987).

- Some children with disabilities have not mastered self-help behaviors, making it difficult to differentiate true cases of neglect.

- To assist some children, touching is required (e.g., lifting, toileting, diapering, bathing, positioning), making accidental touching inevitable and exploitative touching difficult to identify (Garbarino & Authier, 1987).

What Can We Do to Stop Child Abuse?

To stop child abuse, we must know what causes it. Unfortunately, we do not have a definitive answer to its cause. Several theories concerning the etiology of abusive behavior have evolved over time. These theories can be summarized as representing four models:

- Psychiatric Model: The abuser is considered the primary cause of abuse as a result of some neurotic and psychotic disorder.

- Sociological Model: Family, community, and cultural values contribute to abusive behavior in society, with individual and family stress being viewed as the primary cause of abuse.

- Social-Situational Model: Parent-child interaction patterns facilitate and maintain abusive behaviors.

- Ecological Model: Characteristics of the individual, family, community, and social-cultural environment all interact to contribute to abuse (Watkins & Bradbard, 1982; Zirpoli, Snell, & Loyd, 1987).

Each model offers a focus for studying the nature of child abuse. In addition, each model posits certain factors assumed to be related to abuse. Knowledge of these factors can help us prevent and control child abuse.

Familial Factors and Child Characteristics

Over the past two decades, researchers have looked to family variables as possible indicators of potential abuse. Generally, we know little about what causes a parent to abuse a child. What we do know is that some factors are associated with families who abuse their children.

- *Abusers tend to have been abused by their parents* (Egeland, Jacobvitz, & Papatola, 1984, as reported in Zirpoli, 1990; Straus, 1983).

- *Abusers tend to believe that physical punishment and slapping are appropriate behaviors* (Straus, 1980).

- *Abusers are not subjected to significantly more stressful life experiences; however, they tend to perceive that they are more overwhelmed by the stress that they do experience and they tend to associate violence as a response to stress* (Rosenberg & Reppucci, 1983; Starr, 1983; Straus, 1980; Wolfe, 1985).

- *Some abusers of young children place unrealistic demands on them* (Galdston, 1965; Steele & Pollock, 1968).

- *Although males tend to be abusive more often than females, mothers are more likely than fathers to inflict serious injury on a child* (Johnson & Showers, 1885; Solomon, 1973).

- *Abusers tend to experience a high degree of social isolation, as well as fail to use existing social supports* (Garbarino, 1982; Kirkham, Schinke, Schilling, Meltzer, & Norelius, 1986; Salzinger, Kaplan, & Artemyeff, 1983; Young, 1964).

In addition to focusing on family factors, researchers have considered child characteristics. Though it is clear that abused children should never be blamed for the maltreatment that they receive from parents or caretakers, certain characteristics place the child at higher risk of abuse:

- Prematurity or low birth weight (Fontana, 1971; Klein & Stern, 1971; Lynch & Roberts, 1982).

- Difficult temperament, presence of challenging or aggressive behaviors, or behavior disorders (Bousha and Twentyman, 1984; Rusch, Hall, & Griffin, 1986; Zirpoli, Snell, & Loyd, 1987).

- Mental disabilities (Elmer, 1967; Martin, 1972; Nesbit & Karagianis, 1982; Sandgrund, Gaines, & Green, 1974).

The extent to which these characteristics might place the child at risk for abuse is unclear; but the fact is that children with these characteristics require special or additional parental care and attention (Zirpoli, 1986).

Factors Contributing to the Vulnerability of Children with Disabilities

The Child Abuse Prevention, Adoption and Family Service Act of 1988 contains specific mandates that direct efforts to protect children with disabilities from abuse and neglect. Are children with disabilities more at risk?

Research does not conclusively place children with disabilities at higher risk for abuse nor clearly indicate the prevalence of disabilities caused by abuse (West, Leconte, & Cahn, 1988). As Zirpoli (1990) asserted, whether a child's disability is directly or indirectly related to abusive treatment will probably be an ongoing topic for future research.

Research tells us that children who require special attention and extraordinary care may be subject to increased risk for abuse. Families with multiple problems, or limited financial, cognitive, emotional, or social resources, may be at higher risk for neglect because of their inability to attend to all of their child's special health care needs (Jaudes

& Diamond, 1985). In addition, Glaser and Bentovim (1979) found that disabilities in children present a potential for long-term stress. In their study of 111 abused children, 32% of children without disabilities were abused after the age of 2 years compared with 52% of the children with disabilites; only 9% of abused children without disabilities were abused after the age of 5 compared with 29% of children with disabilities.

Although the disability itself does not cause abuse, it can contribute to mistreatment (Zantal-Weiner, 1987). As Mayer and Brenner (1989) summarized, characteristics found in abused children such as excessive or high-pitched crying, unresponsiveness, and toileting problems, are also often associated with children with disabilities; and parent characteristics such as poor parenting skills, unrealistic expectations, inability to cope with stress, marital difficulties, and low self-esteem are also associated with both risk for abuse and parenting a child with disabilities.

The nature of the disability in itself makes the child more vulnerable when the potential for abuse is imminent. According to a report prepared by the Parent Advocacy Coalition for Educational Rights (1986), children with disabilities may be at risk for abuse when they are:

- less able to physically defend themselves
- less able to articulate occurrence of abuse
- unable to differentiate between appropriate and inappropriate physical contact, whether violent or sexual
- more dependent on others for assistance or care
- reluctant to report instances of abuse for fear of losing vital linkages to major care providers

Any one of these characteristics does not in itself lead to abuse, but each can be seen as potentially contributing to abuse. The presence of these characteristics makes the child more vulnerable to becoming abused by a parent, family member, or caretaker because the child's ability to protect himself or herself is compromised or limited by the disabling characteristic.

When Child Abuse Causes Disabilities

A major difficulty in studying maltreatment in populations with disabilities is to determine if the impairment preceded the abusive episode(s), or if it was a consequence of abuse and neglect (Ammerman, Van Hasselt, & Hersen, 1988). Hollohan (1987), testifying before the Senate Subcommittee to reauthorize the Child Abuse and Protection Act of 1974, stated that in 1977 Sternfeld estimated that 12.5% of new cases of cerebral palsy each year in the United States are caused by child abuse.

He went on to point out that in 1979 Buchanan and Oliver found that at least 3% and perhaps as much as 11% of the mental retardation in their study was the result of violence.

Diamond and Jaudes (1983) found that abuse was the cause of cerebral palsy in at least 9.3% of their sample. In 1985, United Cerebral Palsy (Cohen & Warren, 1987) surveyed 42 affiliates serving 2,771 children with developmental disabilities in preschool programs and found that 11.9% acquired the disability as a result of known abuse, with 12.3% resulting from possible abuse.

Physical disabilities and related health problems have resulted from abuse and neglect. Mullins (1986) summarized the following:

- Abused children may suffer permanent physical and mental impairment as a result of physical violence (Brown, 1974).

- Some forms of child abuse in infants can lead to brain damage and mental retardation (Caffey, 1974).

- The central nervous system can be harmed (Holter, 1979; Klein, 1980; Mayer, Walker, Johnson, & Matlak, 1981).

- As a result of severe shaking and jerking, infants can experience brain injury, anterior hypopituitarism, impaired growth, and diabetes insipidus (Miller, Kaplan, & Grumbach, 1980).

There are other potential outcomes of abuse. Fatout (1990) found that abused children had difficulty developing and sustaining relationships. In a study of children who had been sexually abused, 25% of the sample were receiving their education in classrooms for the emotionally disturbed (Soeffing, 1975). Failure to develop appropriate language skills was another outcome identified by Allen and Wasserman (1985).

Other researchers have suggested that abuse may cause learning disabilities (Caplan, Watters, White, Parry, & Bates, 1984; Frisch & Rhoads, 1982). The theory is that in some cases child abuse may impair cognitive development and functioning and, as such, interfere with the child's academic experience. However, as Caplan and Dinardo (1986) concluded in their review of research investigating a possible link between learning disabilities and child abuse, though the research does not support a consensus about the relationship between child abuse and learning disabilities, it seems reasonable to assume that cause-and-effect relationships between the two may exist in individual cases and that the directions of these relations may vary.

Summary

The factors leading to child abuse are complex. The literature often raises more questions than it answers; and given our urgency to stop the continuing harm inflicted on children, we must discover causes so that we can develop solutions now.

Part of the problem with ending child abuse is that child abuse is a response to something. That "something" can range from the abuser's inability to deal with stress to his or her lack of training in more humane or child-centered disciplinary procedures. There is a qualitative difference between the parent who in a drunken stupor throws the child and everything else down the stairs for being in the way and the parent who believes that whipping a child with a belt is an appropriate and necessary disciplinary technique. Because there are multiple sources of child abuse, finding one set of factors that can be manipulated in such a way as to stop the harm is impossible.

As educators approach intervention, we must keep in mind that there are many ethical, as well as practical issues that cloud our ability to identify and prevent child abuse and neglect. These issues should not in any way preclude our efforts on behalf of children, but they pose a caution in the zeal—and legitimacy—of our actions.

3. Implications for Practitioners

Educators are in a unique position to identify and report behaviors symptomatic of abuse and neglect. Variations in state laws and reporting requirements result in variations in districts' referral processes.

Educators' Roles

It is not a new phenomenon for social maladies to find their way into the growing list of school responsibilities. Because it is estimated that over 50% of all children who are abused are of school age (National Center on Child Abuse and Neglect, 1984), educators are in a unique position to identify and report behaviors symptomatic of abuse or neglect. Educators often know immediately when something is not quite right with a child. Properly prepared educators can compare and contrast behaviors that are unusual with those that are not. They can help the child who has been abused better adjust to the classroom, as well as provide opportunities that can help to prevent future occurrences of maltreatment.

Although social service agencies generally have primary responsibility for child abuse control, legislatures have required all professionals with responsibility for children, including educators, to discover and report suspected abuse. In fact, administrators and teachers can face possible charges for failure to report suspected abuse or neglect

Bridgeland & Duane, 1990; McClare, 1990). However, schools do not have the responsibility to prove that a child has been a victim of maltreatment.

All 50 U.S. states have statutes mandating that child abuse be reported. Unfortunately, states differ not only in their definitions of abuse, but also in such matters as who is required to report suspected cases. This variation not only affects prevalence and incidence rates, but also prevents standardized reporting procedures. Thus, it is left to districts to develop a well-organized and delineated referral process that both promotes the rights of children and families, and protects the rights of teaching and administrative staff (see Section 4, "Implications for Program Development and Administration").

Given the overrepresentation of students with disabilities who are abused, special educators must be even more diligent in developing identification procedures and preventive interventions. To accomplish these goals, special educators will need skills in collaborating with other professionals, knowledge of law and child abuse characteristics, and knowledge of programs.

Recognizing Abuse and Neglect

Because child abuse definitions vary by state and locality, the first step for educators is to ascertain the legal definition of child abuse in their state. This definition should form the basis for all school identification and reporting procedures. Districts can support this process by disseminating to their staff specific concrete definitions, which have been developed by both legal counsel and school officials.

District-based training in how to recognize child abuse and neglect is also warranted, especially in light of the research showing that over 30% of teachers received *no* preservice information on the topic; yet teachers constitute the front line in identifying suspected cases (McIntyre, 1987). Additional support for training comes from a study conducted by Volpe (1981), who compared teachers' knowledge of child abuse with other educational support personnel, and found them to be the group least informed and least prepared to respond to cases of suspected child abuse. These studies are not to suggest that teachers are intentionally uninformed about the problem; indeed, McIntyre (1990) found teachers empathic to the needs of abused children and desiring to help. These studies indicate that training is needed to significantly increase knowledge and confidence among key educators regarding abuse and neglect. Possible topics of concern might include definitions, incidence figures, signs and symptoms, parent and child characteristics, legal requirements, reporting procedures, documentation of information, or guidelines for exploring one's own beliefs regarding discipline and abuse or neglect (McIntyre, 1990).

13

Many educational groups and national organizations have developed training materials and inservice programs to assist educators in developing expertise in recognizing, reporting and responding to child abuse. For example, the National Education Association (NEA) and its state and local affiliates have developed a national program for teachers and parents on how to detect abuse and to encourage reporting of abuse (for a description, see Ohman, 1988). The Council for Exceptional Children has published a manual and filmstrip on the prevention and treatment of child abuse (1979). A sampling of other training programs and curricula is found in annotated bibliographies produced by the National Clearinghouse on Child Abuse and Neglect (1991a, b). (See also the "Resources" section of this book.)

At a minimum, educators should familiarize themselves with both the physical and behavioral indicators of each form of child abuse and neglect (Zirpoli, 1986). Sensitive educators can be instrumental in identifying a particular type of maltreatment through the child's appearance or behavior at school. When applying these indicators to students with disabilities, however, it is important to keep in mind that some characteristics of abuse are characteristics associated with disabilities—for example, wariness of adult contact, behavioral extremes, unusual dressing habits, and conduct disorders have been associated with disabilities (Mayer & Brenner, 1989).

Figure 1 summarizes physical and behavioral indicators for physical abuse, physical neglect, sexual abuse, and emotional maltreatment.

Physical Abuse. Whenever an injury is inconsistent with the history given of it, a nonaccidental injury might be inferred. For example, it is highly unlikely that a child would accidentally suffer multiple cigarette burns or multiple bruises to the same location on a regular basis. Some of the most common indicators of nonaccidentally acquired physical injuries include:

- evidence of repeated injury, sometimes before old injuries are healed
- frequent complaints of abdominal pain
- evidence of bruises, especially of different ages; welts; wounds, cuts, or punctures; scalding liquid burns, especially those with well-defined parameters; caustic burns; frostbite; and burns, especially apparent cigarette burns on the back of the neck, head or extremities (Kline, 1977)

Additional indicators include human bite marks and unexplained fractures (National Center on Child Abuse and Neglect, 1984).

FIGURE 1
Physical and Behavioral Indicators of Child Abuse and Neglect

Type of Abuse or Neglect	Physical Indicators	Behavioral Indicators
Physical Abuse	Unexplained Bruises and Welts: – on face, lips, mouth – on torso, back, buttocks, thighs – in various stages of healing – clustered, forming regular patterns – reflecting shape of article used to inflict (electric cord, belt buckle) – on several different surface areas – regularly appear after absence, weekend, or vacation Unexplained Burns: – cigar, cigarette burns, especially on soles, palms, back, or buttocks – immersion burns (sock-like, glove-like, doughnut shaped on buttocks or genitalia) – patterned like electric burner, iron, etc. – rope burns on arms, legs, neck, or torso Unexplained Fractures: – to skull, nose, facial structure – in various stages of healing – multiple or spiral fractures Unexplained Lacerations or Abrasions – to mouth, lips, gums, eyes – to external genitalia	Wary of Adult Contacts Apprehensive When Other Children Cry Behavioral Extremes: – aggressiveness, or – withdrawal Frightened of Parents Afraid to Go Home Reports Injury by Parents
Physical Neglect	Consistent Hunger, Poor Hygiene, Inappropriate Dress Consistent Lack of Supervision, Especially in Dangerous Activities or Long Periods Unattended Physical Problems or Medical Needs Abandonment	Begging, Stealing Food Extended Stays at School (early arrival and late departure) Constant Fatigue, Listlessness, or Falling Asleep in Class Alcohol or Drug Abuse Delinquency (e.g., thefts) States There Is No Caretaker

15

FIGURE 1 - Continued

Type of Abuse or Neglect	Physical Indicators	Behavioral Indicators
Sexual Abuse	Difficulty in Walking or Sitting	Unwilling to Change for Gym or Participate in Physical Education Class
	Torn, Stained, or Bloody Underclothing	
	Pain or itching in Genital Area	Withdrawal, Fantasy, or Infantile Behavior
	Bruises or Bleeding in External Genitalia, Vaginal, or Anal Areas	Bizarre, Sophisticated, or Unusual Sexual Behavior or Knowledge
	Venereal Disease, Expecially in Preteens	Poor Peer Relationships
		Delinquent or Run Away
	Pregnancy	Reports Sexual Assault by Caretaker
Emotional Maltreatment	Speech Disorders	Habit Disorders (sucking, biting, rocking, etc.)
	Lags in Physical Development	Conduct Disorders (antisocial, destructive, etc.)
	Failure to Thrive	Neurotic Traits (sleep disorders, inhibition of play)
		Psychoneurotic Reactions (hysteria, obsession, compulsion, phobias, hypochondria)
		Behavior extremes: – compliant, passive – aggressive, demanding
		Overly Adaptive Behavior: – inappropriately adult – inappropriately infant
		Developmental Lags (mental, emotional)
		Attempted Suicide

Source: National Center on Child Abuse and Neglect. (1984, September). *The educator's role in the prevention and treatment of child abuse and neglect.* Washington, DC: U.S. Department of Health and Human Services, Administration for Children, Youth, and Families, Children's Bureau.

Certain behaviors may also be associated with physical abuse. These behaviors may exist independent of or in conjunction with physical indicators. Educators should be alert for the child who:

- is extremely wary of physical contact with adults
- becomes apprehensive when other children cry
- demonstrates extremes in behavior—either aggressiveness or withdrawal—which is outside the range of behavior expected for the child's developmental level
- seems frightened of his or her parents or caretaker
- states that he or she is afraid to go home, or cries when it is time to leave
- reports injury by a parent or caretaker (National Center on Child Abuse and Neglect, 1984).

Any one of these behavioral indicators does not in itself signal physical abuse. Rather, these are behavioral indicators that have been associated with physical abuse and, therefore, might signal the need for further investigation.

Neglect. Chronic inattention to the basic needs of the child, including food, clothing, shelter, medical care, or supervision, signals possible neglect. One of the problems with identifying neglect regards differentiating true neglect from culturally acceptable child rearing practices in a given community. In other words, school personnel have been known to use the fact that a child comes from a poverty environment as rationale for not reporting neglect. While there are clearly ethical and practical issues inherent in the decision of whether or not to refer a child, the rule of thumb in questionable cases is to report suspected cases of child neglect, if only to ensure that the child has access to the services that society provides. It may well be that in some cases neglect on the part of parents or caretakers is not an overt act of omission, but rather lack of knowledge regarding available services.

Some of the more common indicators of neglect include:

- evidence of inappropriate clothing for the weather
- torn, tattered, or unwashed clothing
- consistently unbathed
- rejection by other children because of body odor
- need for glasses, dental work, or other health services

- lack of proper nourishment
- listlessness or lethargy (Kline, 1977)

With regard to behavioral indicators, educators should be alert to the child who:

- is begging or stealing food
- constantly falls asleep in class
- rarely attends school
- comes to school early and leaves late
- is addicted to alcohol or other drugs
- engages in delinquent acts such as vandalism or theft
- states that no one is home to care for him or her (National Center on Child Abuse and Neglect, 1984)

Note that before any one of these indicators is identified, it must be observed consistently, over a considerable period of time.

Sexual Abuse. The indicators of sexual abuse or molestation are usually more subtle than those of physical abuse. In fact, frequently sexual abuse is only discovered in the school setting after the child confides in a trusted educator.

The physical signs of sexual abuse include:

- difficulty in walking or sitting
- torn, stained, or bloody underclothing
- complaints of pain or itching in the genital area
- bruises or bleeding in external genitalia, vaginal, or anal areas
- venereal disease, particularly in children under 13
- pregnancy, especially in early adolescence (National Center on Child Abuse and Neglect, 1984)

Sexually abused children may also display one or more of the following behaviors:

- appear withdrawn, engage in fantasy or infantile behavior, or appear retarded
- have poor peer relationships
- be unwilling to change for gym or to participate in physical activities

- engage in delinquent acts, or run away

- display bizarre, sophisticated, or unusual sexual knowledge or behavior

- state that he or she has been sexually assaulted (National Center on
Child Abuse and Neglect, 1984)

According to Kline (1977), children who identify sexual contact as a
positive reinforcer for attention may adopt seductive behaviors with
peers and other adults.

Emotional Maltreatment. This type of abuse is perhaps the most difficult
to identify, because the behavior of emotionally maltreated children is
similar to that of children with emotional or behavioral disorders. Also,
though emotionally maltreated children are not always physically
abused, physically abused children are almost always emotionally
maltreated.

Emotional maltreatment is characterized by a persistent lack of
concern evidenced by blaming, belittling, or rejecting a child (National
Center on Child Abuse and Neglect, 1984). Physical indicators include
speech disorders, lags in physical development, and the failure-to-thrive
syndrome. There is no simple list of symptoms to alert educators to the
presence of psychological maltreatment (Garbarino, 1987a), but
Broadhurst's (1986) "signs" in relation to other factors might be helpful
in the beginning of the assessment process:

- shows extremes in behavior

- is either inappropriately adult or infantile

- is delayed physically or emotionally

- has attempted suicide

- reports a lack of attachment to parents

Educators must show caution in associating any one of these factors
with abuse.

Parent Behaviors That Reveal Possible Abuse. In addition to noting signs in
the child, educators can also note parent characteristics that tend to
suggest a "stronger than usual" capability to abuse, neglect, or sexually
molest a child (Kline, 1977). Although no two parents are exactly alike,
they tend to share a combination of characteristics summarized by Kline
(1977, p. 22) as follows:

- expressing fear or showing evidence of losing control
- showing detachment from the child
- giving evidence that he or she is misusing alcohol or drugs
- stating that the child is "injury prone" or has repeated injuries
- stating a strong belief in the value of punishment
- having unrealistic expectations of the child
- being reluctant to give information
- being generally irrational in manner regarding the child's failures
- appearing to be cruel, sadistic, or lacking in remorse when talking about injuries the child has sustained
- having an inappropriate awareness of the child's cognitive, social, and physical needs

In identifying abuse, educators should note any of these behaviors in parents of children suspected of abuse and include a description of them in the case documentation. The educator who knows a child's family is in a better position to gauge whether a problem suggests the possible presence of abuse or neglect.

4. Implications for Program Development and Administration

Steps for establishing effective reporting procedures have been identified. Preventative measures include school programs and support for parents of children with disabilities, preventative programs for students, and measures for preventing institutional abuse and abuse by school staff.

How to Report

Districts should establish reporting systems and make the procedures of these systems known to all staff. According to Switzer (1985), to establish an effective reporting policy, the district should take the following steps:

- Study the most recent version of your state's child abuse reporting statute.

- Contact school systems of similar size in your state to find out what policies and procedures they are using and would recommend.

- Work with your school attorney and local child protection agencies to ensure that your policies not only comply with the law, but can be easily implemented.

In 1976, the Education Commission of the States identified critical elements that should be included in school reporting procedures. The elements the Commission recommended citing included:

- a brief rationale for involving school personnel in reporting

- the name and appropriate section of the state reporting statute

- who specifically is mandated to report and who else may report

- reportable conditions as defined by state law

- the person or agency to receive the reports

- the information required by the reporter

- expected professional conduct by school employees

- the exact language of the law to define "abuse" and "neglect"

- the method by which school personnel are to report and the time in which to report

- whether or not there is immunity from civil liability and criminal penalty for those who report or participate in an investigation or judicial proceeding

- penalty for failure to report, if established by state law

- action taken by school board for failure to report

- any provisions of the law regarding the confidentiality of records of suspected abuse or neglect

In addition to a reporting policy, official reporting forms are beneficial. Official reporting forms provide evidence that the individual and school have complied with the law in reporting suspected abuse or neglect, provide case information and tangible evidence, and establish that the school policies and procedures have been carried out (Kline, 1977). These forms include the following elements:

- names and addresses of the child and parents or caretakers

- child's age

- observations leading to the suspicion that the child is a victim of child abuse or neglect

- nature and extent of the abuse or neglect

- any other helpful information (Wilson, Thomas, & Schuette, 1983)

A sample reporting form is found in Figure 2.

Teachers in districts where there are not formal reporting procedures in place are still obligated by law to refer suspected child abuse cases to the state social service agency in charge of referrals. According to McIntyre (1990), teachers can protect the rights of the child, as well as their own rights, by observing the following procedures:

- Obtain other witnesses to document observed symptoms.

- Keep a personal record documenting objective observations.

- Report the incident, and even if it is anonymously made, record the date and time of the report.

- Follow up with the social service agency to ensure that action has been taken.

After the report is filed, social services and other legally designated parties take over responsibility for the case. It is not the responsibility of the referring educator to prove that abuse exists, nor is it the educator's responsibility to treat the child. Being "cut off" from the process at this point, especially considering that in most cases the child is still the educational responsibility of the educator, can prove very frustrating.

Bridgeland and Duane (1990) found that after referring a child for suspected abuse, teachers experienced frustration with the initial intervention, the lack of feedback they received, and the possibly damaging disposition of abuse cases. To remedy this situation, McIntyre (1990) stressed the need to provide teachers with feedback regarding the status of referral so that they feel their efforts were not ignored or in vain. He also suggested the establishment of a multidisciplinary child study team that interacts with other community organizations such as police, medical facilities, parent-teacher organizations, and social service agencies as a strategy for increasing feedback and communication.

In addition, Bridgeland and Duane (1990) found that teachers who have reported a suspected child abuse case welcome the opportunity to talk to their administrator about their concerns. These researchers suggested the need for ongoing consultation, as well as reassurance that progress was being made on the child's behalf.

FIGURE 2
Sample Child Abuse-Neglect Reporting Form

Child Abuse-Neglect Reporting Form

Oral Report Made to principal or designee: Date _____ Time _____

Child's name _____ / _____ / _____
             Last name (legal)   First   Middle

Age _____ Birthday _____ Sex _____

Child's address _____

Names and addresses of parents or other person(s) responsible for the child's care.

Father _____ Mother _____

Guardian or caretaker _____

Address _____ Telephone _____

Observations leading to the suspicion that the child is a victim of abuse or neglect. (Use Appendix A when answering this question.) Supply time and date of observation(s).

Additional information. Interview with the child and name of other school employees involved.

Written report made to principal or designee: Date _____ Time _____

Signature _____ Signature _____
         Initiator of the report   Observer of the interview

To be filled out by the principal or designee:

Oral report made to: Written report made to:

Local City Police	_____	Local City Police	_____
County Sheriff	_____	County Sheriff	_____
Division of Family Services	_____	Division of Family Services	_____

Date _____ Time _____   Date _____ Time _____

Principal's signature _____

Distribute copies: 1. Mail to agency receiving the oral report.

                     2. Mail to the district's pupil personnel office.

                     3. Place in principal's child abuse-neglect file. (Not to be placed in child's personal file.)

Source: Kline (1977), p. 34.

Prevention: School Programs for Parents

Parents of children with disabilities often experience undue stress making attention to their needs even more critical in our goal of preventing maltreatment of children (Mullins, 1986). Although it has been documented that rearing a child with disabilities can place the family at risk for a host of psychological and emotional problems, including abuse and neglect, recent evidence suggests that many of the negative consequences can be prevented or lessened if the family is provided support that strengthens well-being and family integrity (Dunst, Cooper, & Bolick, 1987). Primary child abuse prevention programs that enhance competencies of families, and prevent the onset of abusive behavior can be targeted to high-risk groups undergoing the transition to parenthood (Rosenberg & Reppucci, 1985).

West, Leconte, and Cahn (1988) identified several service and intervention approaches that have particular relevance to parents of children with disabilities. They suggest tailoring the following strategies to meet the special situations faced by parents of such children:

- Early identification and assessment of children with disabilities can reduce the risk of subsequent abuse and neglect. Provision of services, information, and support to parents can reduce parental isolation and enhance parent-child relationships (Camblin,1982).

- Parent-child bonding is critical to the prevention of abuse and neglect. Because bonding may be interrupted for children with disabilities and their parents, educators can support and strengthen the relationship by providing specialized information to the parent

- Child-management training for parents of children with disabilities may be helpful, because parents who are successful with their children find parenting less stressful.

- Counseling for parents of children with disabilities may be helpful in identifying and addressing stress- and anxiety-producing issues

- Providing social support systems for parents of children with disabilities can help reduce isolation and provide a support network.

Some cases of child abuse and neglect have been associated with the parent's lack of knowledge about children's needs and development. Programs that have been designed to address this need stress the skills required in being a parent and address topics such as nutrition, consumer affairs, family planning, discipline, and budgeting (Marion, 1982). Participants also generally receive instruction about the normal growth and development of a child. High school courses on parenting (family planning, effective parenting, child development, nutrition, management of stress, and selection of child care) can be enhanced with the addition of a practicum in which students interact with young children (McIntyre, 1990).

This type of parenting program has most often been targeted at high school students, but school districts can expand this concept through their adult education programs. Other school-based programs and services that indirectly assist parents include parent education programs that focus on parenting skills; early childhood programs that teach parents about child development and realistic levels of expectations; counseling programs to enhance employment opportunities; and high school completion courses. Because lack of successful coping skills, a reduced ability to ask for and accept help, and a low level of self-sufficiency have been cited as characteristics common to abusive parents, programs that help adults deal with stress and develop life skills can also be helpful.

Schools can also assist parents by serving as a "hub" for services. Through school programs, children can receive free or reduced-priced meals. With the help of school officials, arrangements can be made for glasses, hearing aids or prosthetic devices, and clothing. Extended school days can provide day care and student tutoring opportunities.

Unfortunately, there are obstacles to providing any of these services at a district level. Obstacles to providing preventive services include:

- shortage of fiscal and human resources

- definitional problems concerning what constitutes abuse and neglect, making entitlement difficult

- lack of information about impact of services

- societal value of separation of school and family, individualism and self-sufficiency, and a tradition of noninterference in the affairs of families on the part of schools

- lack of national policy to support prevention (Miller, 1981)

In any case, districts can begin at a basic level by providing parents with information, even if this is only on a day-to-day basis. In the case of parents of children with disabilities, educators should balance information provided to parents about their children's disabilities with information about their children's strengths—educators must help parents see beyond their children's disabilities (Zirpoli, 1986). We should give parents positive feedback, thereby enhancing the image of the child (McIntyre, 1990).

Preventive Programs for Students

Teachers and curriculum leaders should include information on abuse and neglect in required student courses. At the elementary school level, this might involve instruction for self-protection and assertiveness training. This type of training should continue through the senior high school experience. As with any instructional approach or curriculum, materials must be tailored to the strengths and weaknesses of the student group.

For young children, efforts to prevent sexual abuse can be facilitated by teaching children how to touch and be touched (Borkin & Frank, 1986). When educating children about sexual abuse, Borkin and Frank suggested that you stress the following points:

- Establish the concept of private areas of the body that children have a right to control.

- Differentiate between touching that is OK and touching that is not OK.

- Give children permission and right to say no to an adult who is doing something wrong.

- Encourage children to trust their own feelings.

- Instruct children to tell someone if touched inappropriately and to keep telling until someone believes their report.

Tharinger and colleagues (1990) also stressed the importance of providing individuals with mental retardation developmentally appropriate education about their sexuality. The importance of this cannot be understated. As Sobsey and Varnhagen (1989) argued, our current training practices in special education, which place no emphasis on providing sex education and heavy emphasis on compliance with adults, may in fact increase the vulnerability of students with mental retardation. Shaman (1986) found that in nearly 99% of the cases involving sexual exploitation of a person with disabilities, the victim knew the perpetrator. Offenders often manipulate and coerce the individual to expect that no one will believe him or her; thus, prevention programs must also emphasize that the child's disclosures will be believed.

According to Dunst and colleagues (1987), the aversive behaviors manifested by some children with disabilities can constitute a source of stress to the family. Consequently, a promising approach to preventing maltreatment is to decrease or extinguish the occurrence of the particular behaviors that the parents find difficult. Special educators, with their background in behavior management, are in a unique position to offer support along these lines.

Strategies for Supporting Child Abuse Victims

For children who are victims of emotional or psychological maltreatment, Garbarino (1987a) suggested that schools perform three functions:

- Monitoring the mental health of children: Educators can observe problems in intellectual functioning, social competence, and emotional development long before other agencies have access to the child.

- Providing a psychologically positive climate: Educators can actively create a climate that bolsters self-esteem and presents a model of nurturance.

- Offering compensatory interventions: In collaboration with other agencies, schools can act as therapeutic agents.

When Talking to the Child. Should abuse or neglect be suspected, school officials may decide that it is necessary to talk with the child. Or, the child may seek out a trusted educator to talk with. Should the situation arise when you find yourself talking to the child concerning possible inflicted injury or neglect, it is important to observe certain safeguards:

- Do not ask child to remove any clothing.

- Do not overwhelm the child with questions.

- Reassure the child that he or she is not in trouble and has done nothing wrong.

- If the child wants to terminate the conversation, explain that you understand that you are making him or her uncomfortable and can talk later.

- If the child reveals that he or she has been abused, do not appear surprised or horrified, and do not make any remarks about parents; rather, provide support for the child (e.g., "It took courage for you to tell me this.").

- Ask the child's permission to invite another party to the interview (Hurwitz, 1985).

If you do interview the child, immediately follow up with a conference with the principal, counselor, or designated person.

Communicating with the Parents. Although it is never appropriate for an educator to contact a parent in an effort to "prove" a case of maltreatment, there may be times when contact for other reasons related to suspected abuse might be appropriate. For example, the educator might communicate with the family in order to get to know the family situation. Here the emphasis is on obtaining a better understanding of the family dynamics, not on finding fault.

In some districts, the administrator may be designated as the school contact in cases of suspected child abuse. When a report has been filed, he or she may be responsible for contacting the parents or caretakers and informing them about the report.

Parents and caretakers may be apprehensive or angry at the prospect of talking with the school about a report that has been filed on behalf of their child. Though it is important to make the parents or caretakers feel as comfortable as possible, it is also important to communicate the seriousness of the matter and the legal authority for the action. The rule of thumb is to be professional, direct, and honest. Here are some suggestions to consider when meeting with a parent or caretaker:

- Conduct the conference in private.
- Inform the parents or caretaker in the very beginning why the discussion is taking place.
- Make clear any actions that have taken place (e.g., a report filed) and what will happen in the future.
- Assure parents or caretakers of confidentiality when it is warranted, and let them know when something will be passed along to a third party.
- Do not betray the child's confidence to the parents or caretakers.
- Stick to the facts and avoid judging or blaming (National Center on Child Abuse and Neglect, 1984).

Increasingly, schools are making it a common practice to notify parents or caretakers when a report of suspected child abuse and neglect has been filed by a staff member. Keep in mind that regardless of the current situation's outcome, it is likely that you will continue to educate the child; thus it is important for you above all to communicate support for the parents or caretakers, letting them know of your continued interest in their child's well being.

Preventive Programs to Avoid Child Abuse on School Grounds

Increasingly, schools and institutions are being cited for abuse. School officials can help minimize the possibility that staff will engage in misconduct by taking measures such as screening employees, adopting and publishing a code of ethics and complaint procedures for students and parents to use to bring cases of questionable staff conduct to the attention of appropriate district officials, and making clear disciplinary procedures for staff in substantiated cases.

There are also related risks involved when school staff demonstrate care through touching (Bridgeland & Duane, 1990). Some districts are advising their staff to keep their doors open when talking to a child, discouraging any touching, and encouraging staff to keep a running file as protection should any incident be questioned. Some teachers who must work in vulnerable positions (such as supervisor of the locker room) are also demanding safeguards, such as the presence of more than one adult in the room at any given time.

As was previously pointed out, for some people with disabilities, touching is required, whether it be in the context of toileting, feeding, or lifting. In addition, for some self-abusing students, physical restraints are often called for in ameliorating the harm. In these cases, educators must be clear on the safeguards provided them by the district and see to it that procedures are in place that protect both themselves and the children from potential harm.

Various forms of abuse are particular to institutions. In addition to those previously mentioned, institutional abuse can result from misuse of psychotropic drugs, unreasonable isolation or physical restraint, failure to isolate known or suspected perpetrators in a child's environment, and failure to provide appropriate supervision (Brookhouser, 1987).

Finally, a related issue involves the use of corporal punishment in the school. The use of corporal punishment as a prerogative of school officials has been upheld by the Supreme Court (Garbarino & Authier, 1987), even though a number of national groups, such as The Council for Exceptional Children, have policies opposing corporal punishment; and 22 states, the District of Columbia, and Puerto Rico forbid corporal punishment. It is beyond the scope of this book to discuss the full implications of using corporal punishment as a disciplinary technique. One of the major criticisms leveled against its use, however, is that it sends parents the message that physical harm inflicted on a child is justified and appropriate.

Conclusion

Educators have long served as the symbols of justice and purveyors of care for the world's children. For special educators, whose work is devoted to enriching the lives and protecting the welfare of children with disabilities, child abuse at its very core offends their sensitivity and sensibility. It is an intolerable situation.

The value of special educators' personal commitment must never be underestimated. It is this sense of personal commitment to children that, in fact, holds promise for helping parents and others in society find more appropriate ways to relate, interact, and deal with our children.

Given what we know about child abuse, we can begin now to make changes in national priorities and attitudes. As Zirpoli (1990) asserted, we must advocate for four fundamental changes:

- End acceptance of physical punishment against children.

- Advocate for high-priority status for the nation's children, and ensure that their physical, mental, and emotional needs are protected.

- Ensure that all care givers, regardless of background or income, are provided with the appropriate community support necessary to provide their children with a protective, healthy and enriching environment.

- Provide families of children with disabilities the necessary support to live as a family unit and to participate in all community activities (p. 10).

Child abuse threatens us all. Its effects can linger for a lifetime, undermining the pursuit of a life filled with good health and happiness, and in some cases, leading its victims to commit the same crimes. Any effort taken, no matter how small it might seem, is important in promoting a future that is cruelty free for our children.

References

Allen, R., & Wasserman, G. A. (1985). Origins of language delay in abused infants. *Child Abuse and Neglect, 9*(3), 335–340.

Ammerman, R. T., Van Hasselt, V. B., & Hersen, M. (1988). Maltreatment of handicapped children: A critical review. *Journal of Family Violence, 3*(1), 53–72.

Ammerman, R. T., Van Hasselt, V. B., Hersen, J., McGonigle, J. J., & Lubetsky, M. J. (1989). Abuse and neglect in psychiatrically hospitalized multihandicapped children. *Child Abuse and Neglect, 13*, 335–343.

Birrell, R., & Birrell, J. (1968). The maltreatment syndrome in children: A hospital survey. *Medical Journal of Australia, 2*, 1023–1029.

Borkin, J., & Frank, L. (1986). Sexual abuse prevention for preschoolers: A pilot program. *Child Welfare, 65*(1), 75–82.

Bourne, R. (1981). Child abuse and neglect: An overview. In R. Bourne & E. H. Newberger (Eds.), *Critical perspectives on child abuse.* Lexington, MA: Lexington Books.

Bousha, D. M., & Twentyman, C. T. (1984). Mother-child interactional style in abuse, neglect, and control groups: Naturalistic observations in the home. *Journal of Abnormal Psychology, 93*, 106–114.

Bridgeland, W. M., & Duane, E. A. (1990). Principals as secondary enforcers in child abuse. *Education and Urban Society, 22*(3), 314–324.

Broadhurst, D. (1986). *Educators, schools, and child abuse.* Chicago: National Committee for the Prevention of Child Abuse.

Brookhouser, P. E. (1987). Ensuring the safety of deaf children in residential schools. *Otolaryngology—Head and Neck Surgery, 97*, 361–368.

Camblin, L. (1982). A survey of state efforts in gathering information on child abuse and neglect in the handicapped population. *Child Abuse and Neglect, 6*(4), 465–472.

Caplan, P. & Dinardo, L. (1986). Is there a relationship between child abuse and learning disability? *Canadian Journal of Behavioral Science, 18*(4), 367–380.

Caplan, P., Watters, J., White, G., Parry, R., & Bates, R. (1984). Toronto multi-agency child abuse research project: The abused and the abuser. *Child Abuse and Neglect: The International Journal, 8*, 343–351.

Cohen, S., & Warren, R. D. (1987). Preliminary survey of family abuse of children served by United Cerebral Palsy Centers. *Developmental Medicine and Child Neurology, 29*, 12–18.

Council for Exceptional Children. (1979). *We can help: Specialized curriculum for educators on the prevention and treatment of child abuse and neglect.* Reston, VA: Author.

Diamond, L. J., & Jaudes, P. K. (1983). Child abuse in a cerebral-palsied population. *Developmental Medicine and Child Neurology, 25,* 169–174.

Dunst, C. J., Cooper, C. S., & Bolick, F. A. (1987). Supporting families of handicapped children. In J. Garbarino, P. E. Brookhouser, & K. J Authier(Eds.), *Special children special risks: The maltreatment of children with disabilities.* Hawthorne, NY: Aldinede Gruyter.

Education Commission of the States. (1976). *Educational policies and practices regarding child abuse* (Report No. 85). Denver, CO: Author.

Elmer, E. (1967). *Children in jeopardy: A study of abused minors and their families.* Pittsburgh, PA: University of Pittsburgh Press.

Fatout, M. F. (1990). Consequences of abuse on the relationships of children. *Families in Society, 71*(2), 76–81.

Fontana, V. J. (1971). *The maltreated child.* Springfield, IL: Charles C Thomas.

Frisch, L. E., & Rhoads, F. A. (1982). Child abuse and neglect in children referred for learning evaluation. *Journal of Learning Disabilities, 15*(10), 583–586.

Galdston, O. (1965). Observations on children who have been physically abused and their parents. *Journal of Psychiatry, 122,* 440–443.

Garbarino, J. (1982). *Children and families in the social environment.* New York: Aldine.

Garbarino, J. (1987a). What can the school do on behalf of the psychologically maltreated child and the community? *School Psychology Review, 16*(2), 181–187.

Garbarino, J. (1987b). The abuse and neglect of special children: An introduction to the issues. In J. Garbarino, P. E. Brookhouser, & K. J. Authier (Eds.), *Special children special risks: The maltreatment of children with disabilities.* Hawthorne, NY: Aldinede Gruyter.

Garbarino, J., & Authier, K. J. (1987). The role of educators. In J. Garbarino, P. E. Brookhouser, & K. J. Authier (Eds.), *Special children special risks: The maltreatment of children with disabilities.* Hawthorne, NY: Aldinede Gruyter.

Gil, D. G. (1970). *Violence against children: Physical child abuse in the United States.* Cambridge, MA: Harvard University Press.

Glaser, D., & Bentovim, A. (1979). Abuse and risk to handicapped and chronically ill children. *Child Abuse and Neglect, 3,* 565–575.

ollahan, J. (1987). Testimony on behalf of United Cerebral Palsy Associations, Inc., The Senate Subcommittee on Children, Families, Drugs and Alcoholism, Hearing on The Reauthorization of the Child Abuse and Treatment Act of 1974, April 1, 1987.

urwitz, B. D. (1985). Suspicion: Child abuse. *Instructor, 94*(4), 76–78, 81,125.

eckle, W. G. (1986). Our child protection law: The quagmire continues. *Principal, 62*(3), 7–10.

udes, P. K., & Diamond, L. J. (1985). The handicapped child and child abuse. *Child Abuse and Neglect, 9*, 341–347.

hnson, B., & Morse, H. (1968). Injured children and their parents. *Children, 15*, 147–152.

hnson, C. F., & Showers, J. (1985). Injury variables in child abuse. *Child Abuse and Neglect, 9*, 207–215.

empe, C. H., Silverman, F. N., Steele, B. F., Droegemueller, W., & Silver, H. K. (1962).The battered child syndrome. *The Journal of the American Medical Association, 181*, 17–24.

irkham, M. A., Schinke, S. P., Schilling, R. F., Meltzer, N. J., & Norelius, K. L. (1986). Cognitive-behavioral skills, social supports, and child abuse potential among mothers of handicapped children. *Journal of Family Violence, 1*(3), 235–245.

lein, M., & Stern, L. (1971). Low birth weight and the battered child syndrome. *American Journal of Disabled Children, 122*, 15–18.

line, D. F. (1977). *Child abuse and neglect: A primer for school personnel.* Reston, VA: Council for Exceptional Children.

ynch, M.A., & Roberts, J. (1982). *Consequences of child abuse.* New York: Academic Press.

Marion, M. (1982). Primary prevention of child abuse: The role of the family life educator. *Family Relations, 31*(4), 575–582.

Martin, H. P. (1972). The child and his development. In H. C. Kempe & R. E. Helfer (Eds.), *Helping the battered child and his family.* Philadelphia: J. B. Lippincott.

Mayer, P., & Brenner, S. (1989). Abuse of children with disabilities. *Children's Legal Rights Journal, 10*(4), 16–20.

McClare, G. (1990). The principal's role in child abuse. *Education and Urban Society, 22*(3), 307–313.

McIntyre, T. (1987). Teacher awareness of child abuse and neglect.*Child Abuse and Neglect, 11*(1), 33–35.

McIntyre, T. (1990). The teacher's role in cases of suspected child abuse. *Education and Urban Society, 22*(3), 300–306.

Menolascino, F. J., & McCann, B. M. (1983). *Mental health and mente retardation: Bridging the gap.* Baltimore, MD: University Park Press

Miller, C. C. (1981). Primary prevention of child mistreatment: Meetin, a national need. *Child Welfare, 60*(1), 11–23.

Morse, C. W., Sahler, O. Z., & Friedman, S. B., (1970). A three-yea follow-up study of abused and neglected children. *American Journa of Diseases of Children, 120,* 439–446.

Mullins, J. B. (1986). The relationship between child abuse and handicap ping conditions. *Journal of School Health, 56*(4), 134–136.

National Center on Child Abuse and Neglect. (1984, September). *Th Educator's Role in the Prevention and Treatment of Child Abuse an Neglect.* Washington, DC: U.S. Department of Human Services Office of Human Development Services, Administration fo Children, Youth and Families, Children's Bureau.

National Center on Child Abuse and Neglect. (1988). *Study Finding: Study of National Incidence and Prevalence of Child Abuse and Neglec 1988.* Washington, DC: U.S. Department of Human Services, Offic of Human Development Services, Administration for Childrer Youth and Families, Children's Bureau.

National Center on Child Abuse and Neglect. (1989, March). *Child Abus and Neglect: A Shared Community Concern.* Washington, DC: U.! Department of Health and Human Services, DHHS Publication Nc (OHDS) 89–30531.

National Clearinghouse on Child Abuse and Neglect. (1991a). *Curricul* (annotated bibliography). Washington, DC: Author.

National Clearinghouse on Child Abuse and Neglect. (1991b). *Preventio Programs: Training Materials* (annotated bibliography) Washington, DC: Author.

Nesbit, W. C., & Karagianis, L. D. (1982). Child abuse: Exceptionality a a risk factor. *The Alberta Journal of Educational Research, 28,* 69–76.

Ohman, L. (1988). The NEA: Professional organization and advocate fo teachers. In A. Maney & S. Wells (Eds.), *Professional responsibilitie in protecting children: A public health approach to child sexual abuse* New York: Praeger.

Parke, R. D., & Collmer, C. W. (1975). Child abuse: An interdisciplinar analysis. In E. M. Hetherington (Ed.), *Review of child developmen research* (pp. 509–590). Chicago: University of Chicago Press.

Public Law 100-294. Child Abuse Prevention, Adoption, and Famil Services Act of 1988.

Rosenberg, M. S., & Reppucci, N. D. (1983). Abusive mothers: Perception of their own children's behavior. *Journal of Consulting and Clinica Psychology, 51,* 674–682.

senberg, M. S., & Reppucci, N. D. (1985). Primary prevention of child abuse. *Journal of Consulting and Clinical Psychology, 53*(5), 576–585.

sch, R. G., Hall, J. C., & Griffin, H. C. (1986). Abuse-provoking characteristics of institutionalized mentally retarded individuals. *American Journal of Mental Deficiency, 90,* 618–624.

lzinger, S., Kaplan, S., & Artemyeff, C. (1983). Mothers' personal social networks and child maltreatment. *Journal Of Abnormal Psychology, 92,* 68–76.

ndgrund, H., Gaines, R., & Green, A. (1974). Child abuse and mental retardation: A problem of cause and effect. *American Journal of Mental Deficiency, 79,* 327–330.

aman, E. J. (1986). Prevention programs for children with disabilities. In M. Nelson & K. Clark (Eds.), *The educator's guide to preventing child sexual abuse.* Santa Cruz, CA: Network Publications.

bsey, D., & Varnhagen, C. (1989). Sexual abuse and exploitation. In M. C. Sapo and L. Googen (Eds.), *Special education across Canada.* Vancouver: Center for Human Development and Research.

effing, M. (1975). Abused children are exceptional children. *Exceptional Children, 42*(3), 126–133.

lomon, T. (1973). History and demography of child abuse. *Pediatrics, 51,* 773–776.

inetta, J. J., & Rigler, D. (1972). The child-abusing parent: A psychological review. *Psychological Bulletin, 77,* 296–304.

arr, R. H., Jr. (1983). A research-based approach to the prediction of child abuse. In R. H. Starr, Jr. (Ed.), *Child abuse prediction: Policy implications* (pp. 105–134). Cambridge, MA: Ballinger.

eele, B. F., & Pollock, C. B. (1968). A psychiatric study of parents who abuse infants and small children. In R. E. Helfer & C. H. Kempe (Eds.), *The battered child* (pp. 89–133). Chicago: University of Chicago Press.

traus, M. A. (1980). Stress and physical child abuse. *Child abuse and neglect, 4,* 75–88.

traus, M. A. (1983). Ordinary violence, child abuse and wife beating: What do they all have in common? In D. Finkelhor, R. J. Gelles, G. T. Hotaling, & M. A. Straus (Eds.), *The dark side of families: Current family violence research* (pp. 194–223). Beverly Hills, CA: Sage.

traus, M. A., Gelles, R. J., & Steinmetz, S. K. (1980). *Behind closed doors: Violence in the American family.* New York: Anchor Press.

witzer, J. (1985). Now's the time to reexamine your policy on reporting child abuse. *The American School Board Journal, 172*(11), 41–43.

Tharinger, D., Horton, C. B., & Miller, S. (1990). Sexual abuse and exploitation of children and adults with mental retardation and other handicaps. *Child Abuse and Neglect, 14*, 301–312.

Watkins, H. D., & Bradbard, M. R. (1982). Child maltreatment: An overview with suggestions for intervention and research. *Family Relations, 31*, 323–333.

West, M., Leconte, J., & Cahn, K. (1988). Child abuse and developmental disabilities. *Special Issues*. Seattle, WA: National Resource Institute on Children and Youth with Handicaps.

Wilson, J., Thomas, D., & Schuette, L. (1983). The silent screams: Recognizing abused children. *Education, 104*(1), 100–103.

Wolfe, D. A.(1985). Child-abusive parents: An empirical review and analysis. *Psychological Review, 97*, 462–482.

Young, L. (1964). *Wednesday's children: A study of child neglect and abuse*. New York: McGraw-Hill.

Zantal-Weiner, K. (1987). *Child abuse and the handicapped child. ERIC Digest # E446*. Reston, VA: Clearinghouse on Handicapped and Gifted Children, Council for Exceptional Children, Reston, VA.

Zirpoli, T. J. (1986). Child abuse and children with handicaps. *Remedial and Special Education, 7*(2), 39–48.

Zirpoli, T. J. (1990). Physical abuse: Are children with disabilities a greater risk? *Intervention in School and Clinic, 26*(1), 6–11.

Zirpoli, T. J., Snell, M. E., & Loyd, B. H. (1987). Characteristics of persons with mental retardation who have been abused by care givers. *Journal of Special Education, 21*(2), 31–41.

Resources

tion for Child Protection
24 C Park Road
narlotte, NC 28209
04) 529-1080

ofessional and institutional inquiries only

merican Academy of Pediatrics
1 Northwest Point Boulevard
O. Box 927
k Grove Village, IL 60007
00) 433-9016

r professional and public educational materials, contact the Publica-
ns Department. For information on activities of the AAP Committee
n Child Abuse and Neglect, contact Katherine Sanabria.

merican Bar Association (ABA) Center on Children and the Law
00 M Street, N.W.
uite 200
ashington, DC 20036
02) 331-2250

ofessional and institutional inquiries only.

merican Humane Association
merican Association for Protecting Children
Inverness Drive East
glewood, CO 80112-5117
03) 792-9900
00) 227-5242

ofessional publications and public inquiries regarding child protective
rvices and child abuse and neglect.

American Medical Association
Health and Human Behavior Department
515 North State Street
Chicago, IL 60610
(312) 464-5000

American Public Welfare Association
810 First Street, N.E.
Suite 500
Washington, DC 20002-4267
(202) 682-0100

Association of Junior Leagues
660 First Avenue
New York, NY 10016
(202) 683-1515

For legislative information, contact Public Policy Director; for individua
Junior League programs and child abuse and neglect information, con
tact League Services Department.

Boys and Girls Clubs of America
Government Relations Office
611 Rockville Pike
Suite 230
Rockville, MD 20852
(301) 251-6676

1,100 clubs nationwide serving 1.3 million boys and girls. Offers chil
safety curriculum.

**C. Henry Kempe Center for Prevention and Treatment of Child Abus
and Neglect**
1205 Oneida Street
Denver, CO 80220
(303) 321-3963

Child Welfare League of America
440 First Street, N.W.
Suite 310
Washington, DC 20001
(202) 638-2952

Professional and institutional inquiries only.

Childhelp USA
6463 Independence Avenue
Woodland Hills, CA 91367
Hotline: (800) 4-A-CHILD or (800) 422-4453

Provides comprehensive crisis counseling by mental health professionals for adult and child victims of child abuse and neglect, offenders, parents who are fearful of abusing or who want information on how to be effective parents. The Survivors of Childhood Abuse Program (SCAP) disseminates materials, makes treatment referrals, trains professionals, and conducts research.

Childhelp USA (District of Columbia Office)
5225 Wisconsin Avenue, N.W.
Suite 603
Washington, DC 20015
(202) 537-5193

Contact for information on Federal programs and legislation.

General Federation of Women's Clubs
1734 N Street, N.W.
Washington, DC 20036-2920
(202) 347-3168

300,000 clubs nationwide. Provides child abuse and neglect prevention and education programs, nonprofessional support, and legislative activities. Programs are based on needs of community.

Military Family Resource Center (MFRC)
Ballston Center Tower Three
Ninth Floor
4015 Wilson Boulevard
Suite 903
Arlington, VA 22203
(703) 696-4555

Recommends policy and program guidance to the Assistant Secretary of Defense (Force Management and Personnel) on family violence issues and assists the military services to establish, develop, and maintain comprehensive family violence programs.

National Association of Social Workers
7981 Eastern Avenue
Silver Spring, MD 20910
(301) 565-0333

Professional and institutional inquiries only.

National Black Child Development Institute
1463 Rhode Island Avenue, N.W.
Washington, DC 20005
(202) 387-1281

Provides newsletter, annual conference, and answers public inquirie
regarding issues facing black children and youth.

National Center for Child Abuse and Neglect (NCCAN)
Administration for Children, Youth and Families
Office of Human Development Services
Department of Health and Human Services
P.O. Box 1182
Washington, DC 20013

Responsible for the federal government's child abuse and neglect a
tivities. Administers grant programs to states and organization to furthe
research and demonstration projects, service programs, and other a
tivities related to the identification, treatment, and prevention of chi
abuse and neglect.

Clearinghouse provides selected publications and information service
on child abuse and neglect. (703) 821-2086

National Center for Missing and Exploited Children
2101 Wilson Boulevard
Suite 550
Arlington, VA 22201
(703) 235-3900
(800) 843-5678

Toll-free number for reporting missing children, sightings of missin
children, or reporting cases of child pornography. Provides free writte
materials for the general public on child victimization, as well as technic
documents for professionals.

National Committee for Prevention of Child Abuse
332 South Michigan Avenue
Suite 1600
Chicago, IL 60604-4357
(312) 663-3520

68 local chapters (in all 50 states). Provides information and statistics on child abuse and maintains an extensive publications list. The National Research Center provides information for professionals on programs, methods for evaluating programs, and research findings.

National Council of Juvenile and Family Court Judges
P.O. Box 8970
Reno, NV 89507
(702) 784-6012

Primarily professional and institutional inquiries.

National Council on Child Abuse and Family Violence
1155 Connecticut Avenue, N.W.
Washington, DC 20036
(800) 222-2000

National Crime Prevention Council
1700 K Street, N.W.
2nd Floor
Washington, DC 20006
(202) 466-6272

Provides personal safety curricula, including child abuse and neglect prevention for school children and model prevention programs for adolescents. Educational materials for parents, children, and community groups are available.

National Education Association (NEA)
Human and Civil Rights Unit
1201 16th Street, N.W.
Room 714
Washington, DC 20036
(202) 822-7711

Offers training to NEA members. Sells child abuse and neglect training kits and supplemental materials to professionals and the general public.

National Exchange Club Foundation for Prevention of Child Abuse
3050 Central Avenue
Toledo, OH 43606
(419) 535-3232

Provides volunteer parent aide services to abusive and neglectin
families in 37 cities.

National Network of Runaway and Youth Services
1400 Eye Street, N.W.
Suite 330
Washington, DC 20005
(202) 682-4114

Provides written materials, responds to general inquiries regardin
runaways and adolescent abuse, and serves as a referral source fc
runaways and parents.

National Organization for Victim Assistance (NOVA)
1757 Park Road, N.W.
Washington, DC 20010
(202) 232-6682

Provides information and referral for child victims, as well as crisi
counseling.

National Runaway Switchboard Metro-Help, Inc.
3080 North Lincoln
Chicago, IL 60657
(800) 621-4000 (toll-free)
(312) 880-9860 (business)

Provides toll-free information, referral, and crisis counseling services t
runaway and homeless youth and their families. Also serves as th
National Youth Suicide Hotline.

Parents Anonymous
6733 South Sepulveda Boulevard
Suite 270
Los Angeles, CA 90045
(800) 421-0353 (toll-free)
(213) 410-9732 (business)

1,200 chapters nationwide. National program of professionally facilitatec
self-help groups. Each state has different program components.

Parents United/Daughters and Sons United/Adults Molested as
Children United
232 East Gish Road
San Jose, CA 95112
(408) 453-7616

150 chapters nationwide. Provides guided self-help for sexually abusive
parents as well as child and adult victims of sexual abuse.

Victims of Child Abuse Laws (VOCAL)
2 North Broadway
Suite 133
Santa Ana, CA 92701
(714) 558-0200

National Child Welfare Resource Centers

National Child Abuse and Neglect Clinical Resource Center
Kempe National Center
University of Colorado Health Sciences Center
1205 Oneida Street
Denver, CO 80220
(303) 321-3963

National Child Welfare Resource Center for Management and
Administration
University of Southern Maine
96 Falmouth Street
Portland, ME 04103
(207) 780-4430
(800) HELP-KID

National Legal Resource Center for Child Welfare
American Bar Association
1800 M Street, N.W.
Suite 200
Washington, DC 20036
(202) 331-2250

National Resource Center for Foster and Residential Care
Institute for the Study of Children and Families
Eastern Michigan University
102 King Hall
Ypsilanti, MI 48197
(313)487-0372

National Resource Center for Special Needs Adoption
A Division of Spaulding for Children
3660 Waltrous Road
P.O. Box 337
Chelsea, MI 48118
(313) 475-8693

National Resource Center for Youth Services
The University of Oklahoma
202 West 8th Street
Tulsa, OK 74119-1414
(918) 585-2986

National Resource Center on Child Sexual Abuse
106 Lincoln Street
Huntsville, AL 35801
(205) 533-KIDS
(800) KIDS-006

National Resource Center on Family Based Services
The University of Iowa School of Social Work
Oakdale Campus, N240 OH
Oakdale, IA 52319
(319) 335-4123

National Resource Institute on Children and Youth with Handicaps
Child Development and Mental Retardation Center
University of Washington
Mailstop WJ-10
Seattle, WA 98195
(206) 543-2213

People of Color Leadership Institute
714 G Street, S.E.
Washington, DC 20003
(202) 544-3144

CEC Mini-Library
Exceptional Children at Risk

A set of 11 books that provide practical strategies and interventions for children at risk.

- *Programming for Aggressive and Violent Students.* Richard L. Simps(
  Brenda Smith Miles, Brenda L. Walker, Christina K. Ormsbee,
  Joyce Anderson Downing. No. P350. 1991. 42 pages.

- *Abuse and Neglect of Exceptional Children.* Cynthia L. Warger wi
  Stephanna Tewey & Marjorie Megivern. No. P351. 1991. 44 pag(

- *Special Health Care in the School.* Terry Heintz Caldwell, Barba
  Sirvis, Ann Witt Todaro, & Debbie S. Accouloumre. No. P352. 19(
  56 pages.

- *Homeless and in Need of Special Education.* L. Juane Heflin & Kathr,
  Rudy. No. P353. 1991. 46 pages.

- *Hidden Youth: Dropouts from Special Education.* Donald L. Macmilla
  No. P354. 1991. 37 pages.

- *Born Substance Exposed, Educationally Vulnerable.* Lisbeth J. Vince)
  Marie Kanne Poulsen, Carol K. Cole, Geneva Woodruff, & Dan
  Griffith. No. P355. 1991. 28 pages.

- *Depression and Suicide: Special Education Students at Risk.* Eleanor
  Guetzloe. No. P356. 1991. 45 pages.

- *Language Minority Students with Disabilities.* Leonard M. Baca
  Estella Almanza. No P357. 1991. 56 pages.

- *Alcohol and Other Drugs: Use, Abuse, and Disabilities.* Peter E. Leor
  No. P358. 1991. 33 pages.

- *Rural, Exceptional, At Risk.* Doris Helge. No. P359. 1991. 48 page(

- *Double Jeopardy: Pregnant and Parenting Youth in Special Educatio*
  Lynne Muccigrosso, Marylou Scavarda, Ronda Simpson-Brown,
  Barbara E. Thalacker. No. P360. 1991. 44 pages.

Save 10% by ordering the entire library, No. P361, 1991. Call for the mo
current price information, 703/620-3660.

Send orders to:
The Council for Exceptional Children, Dept. K11150
1920 Association Drive, Reston VA 22091-1589